D0526196

HENNA BODY ART

MARK SMITH

This paperback edition first published in the UK in 2008 by
Haldane Mason Ltd, PO Box 34196, London NW10 3YB

ISBN 978-1-905339-46-4

Printed in China

2 4 6 8 9 7 5 3 1

British Library CIP Data
A catalogue record for this title is available from the British Library

A HALDANE MASON BOOK
Art Director: Ron Samuel
Project Editor: Naomi Waters
Designer: Sarah Collins
Photography pp28, 29: Joff Lee

PICTURE ACKNOWLEDGEMENTS
Trip Photo Library: 4T (B Turner), 4B, 20, 21 (H Rogers), 11T (Dinodia), 13T (M Jelliffe); *Robert Estall Photo Library:* 5 (Carol Beckwith/Angela Fisher), 13 (Angela Fisher); *Panos Pictures:* 6 (D Sansoni), 12T, 12C (John Miles), 17 (Chris Stowers), 22 (Jeremy Horner), 34 (Jean-Léo Dugast); *Werner Forman Archive:* 8, 30; 9 (Philip Goldman Collection); *Robert Harding Picture Library:* 10 (T Gervis), 15, 43 (J H C Wilson), 18 (Visa); *Hutchison Picture Library:* 11C, 40; 14 (Sarah Errington), 25 (Edward Parker), 33 (Christine Pemberton); *Christine Osborne Pictures:* 24.

Every effort has been made to trace the copyright holders and we apologize in advance for
any unintentional errors or omissions. We would be pleased to insert the appropriate
acknowledgement in any subsequent edition of this publication.

WARNING
In rare instances, the application of henna to the skin can cause an allergic reaction. Every
effort has been made to provide full safety and application instructions. The publisher and
copyright holder cannot be held liable for any personal injury suffered through the use of
henna as described in this book.

CONTENTS

Introduction

Henna tattoos have a long history of use in Eastern cultures, particularly in India, Arabia and North Africa, but why is henna so popular today? Some would say that it is simply a fashion trend inspired by celebrities such as Madonna, Liv Tyler, Demi Moore and Prince. Seeing Madonna with henna tattoos on her hands in her video for the single 'Frozen' certainly gave henna a far wider exposure to the media. It became a much talked-about style of body decoration, and as a result, interest in this traditional art form was ignited, spawning a great deal of promotion on television and in glossy magazines.

But the popularity of henna cannot wholly be attributed to its use by celebrities. Henna is still used in Eastern cultures and it was probably only a matter of time before it became accessible in the West. It is a fundamental human urge to use the skin as a canvas for artistic expression. To decorate your own body is the most pertinent expression of individuality and creativity available – be it permanent or not. Tattooing as an art form on the skin has been practised for many thousands of years. Today it is again growing in popularity – as are all forms of body decoration and adornment, such as piercing and the wearing of ethnic jewellery.

Another attraction of henna tattoos is that they are temporary. You can try out different styles and designs without them being permanent or painful, which real tattoos can be. As we all know, fashion changes rapidly, and what is in vogue today may well be out of date tomorrow. With henna you can change your designs as your tastes and fashion demands. It is easy to apply by yourself – or you may like to do it with the help of your friends, especially for the more intricate designs on the hands, or

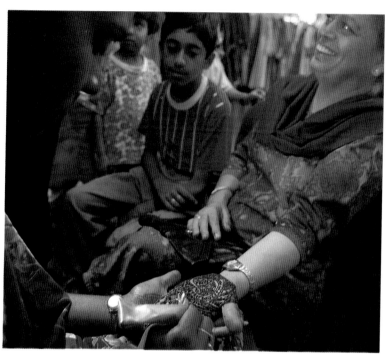

Here a woman is having a henna design applied in a department store in Bangalore.

on areas which are not easily accessible, such as the shoulder.

Henna has become widely available in the late 1990s due to public demand. In major cities you can walk into some stores and have a henna design applied to your skin by a professional, for the right price. Henna will continue to be used in its traditional forms, as well as the more recently developed modern application methods, for many years to come. With the assistance of this book and henna materials, I trust that you will find the art of henna tattooing as fun, easy and creative as the many people all over the world who have taken up this ancient and beautiful art.

What is Henna?

Henna is a dried powder derived from a small shrub whose botanical name is *Laesonia inermis*. It is a member of the Loosestrife family, *Lythraceae,* and grows to a height of between 2.5 and 3 metres. Growing predominantly in hot climates, the henna plant can be found in countries like Iran, India, Pakistan, Egypt, and throughout North Africa. It is also cultivated in China, Indonesia and the West Indies. As a result, it is widely used by the various cultures of all these nations.

The henna leaves are harvested once the plant is in flower. The topmost leaves contain the strongest dye and are used to create the high quality powder used for skin decoration. These leaves will be ground down first to prevent any deterioration of the dye. Then the rest of the leaves

Henna plant growing in Tunisia, with flowers.

from the plant will be dried and ground down; this is the lower-grade powder used in hair dyes and shampoos.

Henna is most widely known in the West as a reddish-brown hair dye that has very good conditioning properties. You may have used one of the many henna shampoos or one with henna extract, which are widely available. Perhaps you have dyed your hair with henna. The popularity of henna in the East spans many

A sack of dried henna leaves for sale.

Veiled Swahili mother with her child, Lamu. The mother's hands are decorated with henna.

centuries. It is used for colouring the hair and fingernails, but its most common form of use is as a skin colourant for body decoration in traditional ceremonies.

In some cultures henna has been used for more than just cosmetic purposes. Henna contains a resinoid substance which has chemical properties that have been used to treat certain ailments. In the past it has been taken internally and applied externally to treat such conditions as cancer of the colon, smallpox, leprosy, headaches,

rheumatic and arthritic pains, and blood loss during labour. This book, however, does not advocate the use of henna for anything other than external cosmetic use.

You may have heard the name *mehndi* (pronounced me-hen-dee) used for henna and henna art, which is the traditional Indian name. Other names include *maruthani* (the Tamil or south Indian name), or *saumer* (the Sudanese name for black henna). For our purposes, it is simplest to refer to it as henna.

THE HISTORY
OF HENNA

Painting from a doorway in Sri Lanka, showing henna body decoration.

Early Uses of Henna

The history and origins of the use of henna are hard to trace. With centuries of migration and cultural interaction, it is difficult to determine which culture and people started using henna first. There is archaeological evidence to suggest that the ancient Egyptians used henna to colour their nails, hair and even their beards: traces of henna have been found on the nails and hair of mummified Pharoahs.

By the time of the Moghul invasion of India in the 16th century AD, henna was widely used throughout North Africa and the Middle East, and this invading force is usually credited with importing the practice into the Indian sub-continent. But Indian cave paintings depicting deities decorated with henna and dating from the fourth and fifth centuries would suggest that it was already in use in the region. Henna

Detail of a painting from the tomb of Nakht, Egypt, *c.* 1421–1413BC.

10

became particularly popular with the inhabitants of Rajasthan who applied henna mixed with aromatic oils to the hands and feet, much the way it is done in India today.

Some people believe that the Chinese were the first to use henna, but so far it can only be traced to the early Christian period in the southern parts of this country. Whatever the case, it is clear that henna has been used by many different cultures for many centuries, even millennia.

Once the use of henna as a form of decoration became more widespread, it developed in its cultural importance and became included in many aspects of daily, spiritual and ceremonial life. When royalty embraced henna as an art form, it secured a place in the the the traditions of India and gradually filtered down through the caste system to become accessible to those from all walks of life. As its popularity grew, so too did the diversity of designs, application methods and recipes.

While henna is often merely decorative and celebratory, religious connotations have also played an important part in its use in both Hindu and Islamic cultures.

Renowned as a lover, Krishna plays with the gopis (cowherds), who have hennaed hands.

Most notably, Hindu deities are decorated with henna tattoos on their hands and feet. This can be seen on wall-paintings and even on statues.

The Prophet Mohammed is believed to have used henna to colour both his hair and beard, a practice that continues to this day. Mohammed also liked his wives to colour their nails with henna. Since Mohammed is seen as the model of perfection whom all Moslems should emulate, his example has guaranteed henna's continuing prominence as a form of body decoration within Islam.

Henna Designs Around the World

Many different regions of the world have used henna body decoration throughout history, and thus it is possible to detect regional variations in the designs of the tattoos as well as the significance attached to them. Designs can mean certain things for certain cultures, such as fertility, good health, wisdom and spiritual enlightenment. Each culture's unique designs have developed through inspiration from individual cultural experience, local architecture, indigenous fabrics and the natural environment of the particular region.

There are three broad distinctive styles which can be defined by geographical area – Asian, Middle Eastern and North African. What unites these cultures in their use of henna is the desire to decorate and beautify the body and the application methods and materials used, thus making henna a truly global form of body decoration.

A girl painting the hands of her friend for a festive occasion in Rajasthan, India.

Asia

The Indian subcontinent has long been regarded as the traditional home of henna body art. The styles of decoration currently in use have been around for centuries, passed down from one generation to the next. Many of the styles cross the political borders between India and Pakistan. Generally, henna art in India uses fine, intricate lines for detail, incorporating lacy, floral designs and paisley patterns, which are used to cover the hands, forearms, feet and shins.

Peculiar to southern India is a style that is used by village elders who draw a circular pattern on the hands and then fill in the centre of the palm with colour. Following this the fingers are 'capped', or completely covered in colour, to finish the design. Capping the fingers is used throughout India and Pakistan

Hand and foot henna decorations from India.

as a design style, a practice which dates back to the earliest uses of henna.

In Indonesia and Malaysia, migration from India and the Middle East has resulted in decorative henna designs being composed of a mixture of the key characteristics of traditional Indian designs and Middle Eastern traits that we shall look at in the next section (see page 14).

The Middle East

Striking and distinctive designs orginating from Yemen.

Designs from the Middle East are usually featured on the hands and tend to be larger, with greater spacing than those on the Indian continent. Floral patterns are commonly used for both the hands and feet. The depiction of flowers, leaves and geometric shapes predominates in this region because of the religious belief that Muslims may not pray with figurative

representations on the body. As a result, and unlike the designs used in Africa, there are no images of human faces, birds or animals in the designs of the Middle East – the same can be said for Pakistan since it is a Muslim country. It is a common practice in the Middle East to complete a hand decoration by dying the fingernails with henna. Henna is most frequently used by Arab brides at their weddings.

14

Africa

Designs from the African continent are quite different from those used in other parts of the world. Patterns tend to be bold, using large geometric designs, with angular lines and often fairly large areas of solid colour. It is common to find the inclusion of religious symbols. Certain tribes have used designs that are developed around either peacock, butterfly, or fish images. Particular attention is also paid to filling in the gaps around the central motif.

This Mali woman has henna around her lips.

A Guerda dancer from Mauritania displays her bold henna designs.

Women from the Berber tribes of North Africa bear a vast number of tattoos and markings that represent certain beliefs and superstitions, passed down from mother to daughter. They are applied with the specific intention of warding off supernatural forces – acting as a talisman to safeguard the health and well-being of the wearer. Berber women tattoo their faces to protect against harmful forces entering through facial orifices. They also paint their feet to protect their bare soles and heels. The pattern prevents hostile forces from working evil magic on the 'soul material' that is left behind in the footprints.

The Use of Henna in Wedding Ceremonies

Decorating parts of the body with henna plays a central role in the wedding ceremonies of many Eastern cultures, from India to Arabia. This involves painting the hands and feet, sometimes extending up the arms and lower leg.

Known as the henna or *mehndi* night, all of the bride's female friends and relatives from both families gather together for a night

A Sudanese woman shows off her hands decorated for her forthcoming marriage.

of celebration and decoration that marks the bride's passing from childhood into the adult world of marriage. The women sing songs, prepare food and, most importantly, they prepare the henna. This preparation culminates in the detailed application of special designs on the bride. The application is generally undertaken by a very close relative or bridesmaid, although nowadays a professional *mehndi* artist may be brought in. Many of the designs reflect sentiments of good fortune, happiness and fertility in the new marriage.

The decorations can also hold references to both sets of in-laws, and even the name of the groom may be incorporated into the design. On the wedding day it is then his task to find his name – a process which may take some time given the extremely intricate nature of the decoration.

16

In some rituals the henna night is so highly regarded that unless the mother-in-law of the bride applies the first dot of henna to the bride's hand the rest of the painting cannot continue. Such a mark is regarded as a symbolic blessing, without which the the bride is not permitted to beautify herself for the groom. A bride's relationship with her mother-in-law is extremely important since she will go to live in the home of her husband's family after the marriage ceremony. Thus the henna night is full of charms and superstition about mothers-in-law; for example, it is widely believed that the deeper the colour of the henna, the more your mother-in-law will love and favour you.

In the Gulf region of the Middle East, the henna night takes place three days before the wedding ceremony, and it bears many similarities to those held in honour of Indian brides. Arab brides have their hands and feet painted while traditional songs are sung by their mothers and grandmothers. Throughout the region, henna decoration is used for many other ceremonial occasions such as births and christenings – anything that involves a celebration, festival or family gathering.

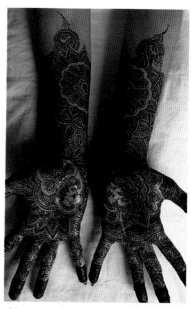

This exquisite decoration from India features the faces of the bride and groom.

It is rare that the groom is involved in the henna night since these are usually women-only affairs, although in some parts of India the groom's hands are decorated. In certain Bangladeshi and Kashmiri communities, designs have been developed especially for men. The groom may come into contact with henna later in life if he decides to use it to colour his hair and beard.

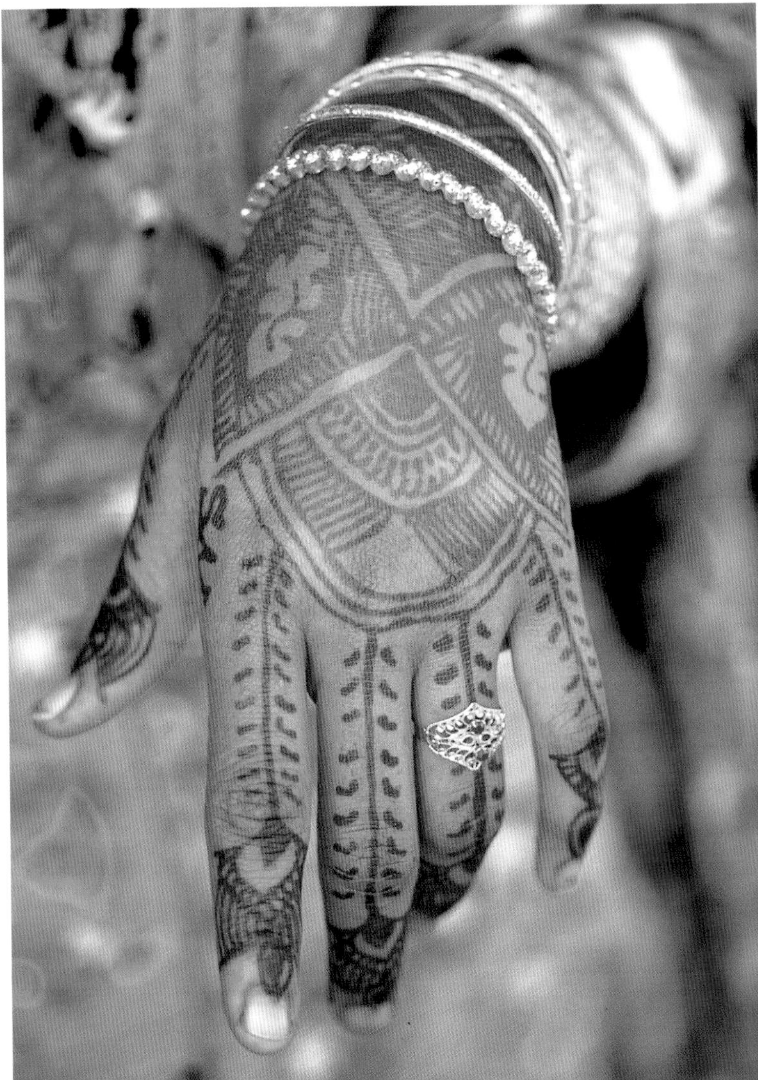

MATERIALS

An intricate geometric hand design from Oman.

Traditional henna provides you with a fantastic effect and is in keeping with the artistic traditions developed and maintained in the East today. But we are not limited to this form; there are several alternatives. Different levels of experience are required for using henna in its different forms. You do not need to be particularly artistic; a steady hand and patience are all you require. Once you have a little more confidence and experience, you may want to try your hand at developing your own henna from powder and special liquids and oils. For the more advanced and adventurous, I have provided some recipes for you to try.

Pre-mixed Henna

Like the one provided in this kit, pre-mixed henna is usually sold in tubes from a wide variety of Asian shops and supermarkets. You may also find this type of henna in specialist outlets and at local street markets. Pre-mixed henna is the best option if you have never tattooed with henna before, since you do not have to spend any time mixing or developing the henna. The consistency is fairly stable so you are free to devote your efforts to application and getting the design correct. Use your pre-mixed henna within a year, applying it in the same way as a cone (see page 33).

Kits of henna in a Tunisian shop.

Henna Powder

This is the basic henna substance that you will need to mix with various other liquids in order to create your own henna paste. The powder is obtained from the ground leaves of the henna plant. Again, it is widely available through Asian shops and markets. Some stage make-up suppliers also stock henna powder, and it is worth discussing your intentions with the staff in these outlets, since they can often give you tips about mixing henna and on the application of the paste. I have picked up some excellent advice from the Indian women who work in my local Asian food shop, all of whom practise the art of henna tattooing.

Some packs contain a couple of sachets or cones of henna powder, *mehndi* oil (usually clove or eucalyptus oil), and some developing liquid (usually a mixture of water and oil). If you find henna powder accompanied by these items, then your task is relatively straightforward.

Berber woman in Tetouan, Morocco, selling henna powder in a market.

This market in India is typical of those where henna powder is sold throughout the East.

How to Make Your Own Henna Paste

1 First of all it is important to sift the henna powder. This will remove any small particles from the plant (such as twigs and stems) which could cause your cone to become blocked. Sifting also gives a much smoother paste.

2 Heat the pouch of developer in boiling water for a few minutes.

3 Add the heated developer liquid to the henna powder and mix thoroughly. If there is room, you can mix them together within the sachet or cone provided, but this may prove fiddly and messy. I recommend that you pour them both into an old bowl to mix properly. Remember to use a bowl that you do not need to use any more; henna is a dye and will stain the bowl. Mix the henna powder and liquid until it reaches the consistency of toothpaste. This consistency will give you the greatest ease of application.

4 Once mixed to toothpaste consistency, cover the paste with cling film and leave it for a minimum of two hours. Some practitioners say it should be kept hot, others that it should be refrigerated. I recommend you keep it in a warm, but not hot, place, such as an airing cupboard.

5 Once the two hours have elapsed, you may need to add a couple of drops of oil to make the paste smooth. This will also help to make the colour stronger. To apply the paste, you can either use a cone or follow the instructions in the next chapter. Don't forget to prepare your skin properly first (see page 35).

A Henna Recipe

It may be that you have only been able to purchase the henna powder by itself, but do not despair! I have a few recipes that have been tried and tested the world over. All of them are simple to prepare and use ingredients that you should have at home. If not, they are very easy to find and inexpensive to buy.

You will need
- Henna powder
- Approx ¼ pint distilled water
- Fresh lemon juice
- Sugar
- Eucalyptus oil
- Tea bags
- Instant coffee
- A fine sieve
- An old bowl

Method

1 Use a good quality henna powder and sieve it two or three times as this will remove any excess particles of the plant. Remember that fine powder equals smooth paste.

2 Boil the distilled water. It is best to use pure water like this because it does not contain any chlorine or other minerals. Add two tea bags to the boiled water and let the mixture infuse. After five minutes, add two teaspoons of instant coffee.

Henna sold in an Arab women's beauty shop.

Hindu make-up and paraphernalia, including henna and stencils for applying to the hands.

3 Remove the tea bags from the liquid. Add at least two tablespoons of fresh lemon juice to the henna powder. Add the water-tea-coffee liquid slowly to the powder, mixing all the time. Just add enough to make the henna paste the consistency of toothpaste, so that it is easy to squeeze through a cone or dab on to the skin.

4 Cover the mixture with cling film and leave in a warm place, such as an airing cupboard, to develop. It should be left for a minimum of two hours, longer if possible.

5 Before use, mix a few drops of eucalyptus oil into the paste. This helps the henna adhere to the skin and deepens the colour.

6 Keep some lemon juice and sugar for applying to the paste once it is on the skin. This helps keep the paste moist and deepens the final colour (see page 41).

7 Your henna paste is now ready to apply using one of the techniques described in the next chapter (see page 31).

Tips and Variations

There are all sorts of things you can do to vary the recipe on the previous page by adding and changing ingredients. Surfing the Internet is a good way to discover methods and recipes used by other henna artists.

26

● A popular and easy variation is simply to leave the henna to develop overnight in the refrigerator, returning it to room temperature before use.

● The following variation is a traditional method from the United Arab Emirates. Follow the directions for the recipe above, but in place of fresh lemon juice, use the boiled juice of dried limes. Cut between three and six limes into slices (this helps them dry quicker) and dry them on a cake rack. Boil the dried limes in the water until the water turns red. Now follow the rest of the recipe above.

This method provides a very dramatic colour, darkening the henna twofold at least. It also helps to stain the skin for longer. Only advance to this method once you have gained some experience in applying henna.

● You can use different types of oil when mixing your own henna, and clove oil is a popular choice. Some people combine this with eucalyptus oil for its pleasant smell. I do not recommend using olive oil, which gives the henna a very unmanageable texture.

● If you have any henna left over after completing your design, you can keep it in the refrigerator for up to a week. To keep it in a reusable condition, it should be stored in an airtight container. You can also freeze henna for up to a month if it is kept in its cone and sealed in an airtight container for absolute freshness.

● While it is traditional in many regions and designs, I do not recommend that you apply henna to your fingernails. The stain will be permanent and will take about six months to grow out completely.

Black Henna

A lot of people have asked me about the use of 'black henna'. I have to agree that the effect of black henna or substances passed off as such do create a very striking and dramatic look. But it is worth remembering that this 'black henna' can be dangerous. In some African countries a black paste of ash and ammonia compounds is applied to the stain left behind once the henna has been brushed off. This will certainly make the tattoo black, but it is also poisonous, and is definitely NOT recommended.

In India, it is possible to purchase black 'henna' powder from traditional markets, but it is not widely available in the West. The usual form of henna is the bright green powder which, when mixed into a paste, does indeed appear black once dried on the skin. Once this has flaked off, however, it will leave behind a lovely, rich, reddish-brown stain, which will last for between two and four weeks.

There are other, safe ways of making your design darker:

● Although time-consuming, you can simply apply the henna three or four times over the same design to achieve greater density of colour.

● In the Sudan, people hold their hands and feet over a smoking fire before brushing off the henna. This practice is called *dukhan*, meaning smoke, and once the henna is removed it leaves the design looking black.

● By far the simplest and safest way of achieving a black henna effect is to use temporary tattoo inks which are described on page 28.

Alternatives to Traditional Henna

It is possible to create the effect of a henna tattoo by using temporary tattoo inks. These are available from many cosmetics and theatrical shops, and from markets, and are the closest thing in appearance to real henna. They are very safe and easy to use, and even easier to remove. The inks come in liquid form and are available in the reddish-brown colour of henna, as well as blue and black. You simply paint these inks on the skin freehand, or you can follow a transfer or stencil, as shown on pages 36–40. It is important to cleanse the skin with alcohol first; you can follow the instructions on page 35.

Temporary tattoo inks are very easy to use and are usually applied with a very fine brush.

Providing a great substitute for henna, these inks are generally waterproof for a couple of days but can easily be removed with baby oil or alcohol. You are therefore not committed to a design for three or four weeks as you are with henna. This is a great way to try out designs to see if you like the effect. They are also very convenient if you are not allowed to wear tattoos at work but want to wear them in your spare time or for special occasions.

When applying these inks, remove any excess ink from the brush by tapping the brush against the side of the bottle prior to use. This prevents the ink 'bleeding' into the fine cracks of the skin.

28

Henna for Children

Henna paste is perfectly safe to use on children, as are the temporary tattoo inks described opposite. Children can easily become restless sitting still in one spot for the length of time it takes to apply a henna tattoo, so it is often easier to use body and face paints to achieve a henna effect.

There are plenty of these on the market; liquid body paints are best, but a pancake of colour is also fine. You just need to choose the right colour, or you could mix a couple of colours to achieve the correct shade of reddish-brown.

The good thing about these types of paints is that most of them are water-based, so children can use them by themselves, and any mess will usually wash off. So when you are busy applying your own traditional henna design, any children that may be present can also be busy mixing colours and creating their own safe and colourful motifs.

Some temporary tattoo kits appear similar to traditional watercolour boxes. The principles of application are much the same, too.

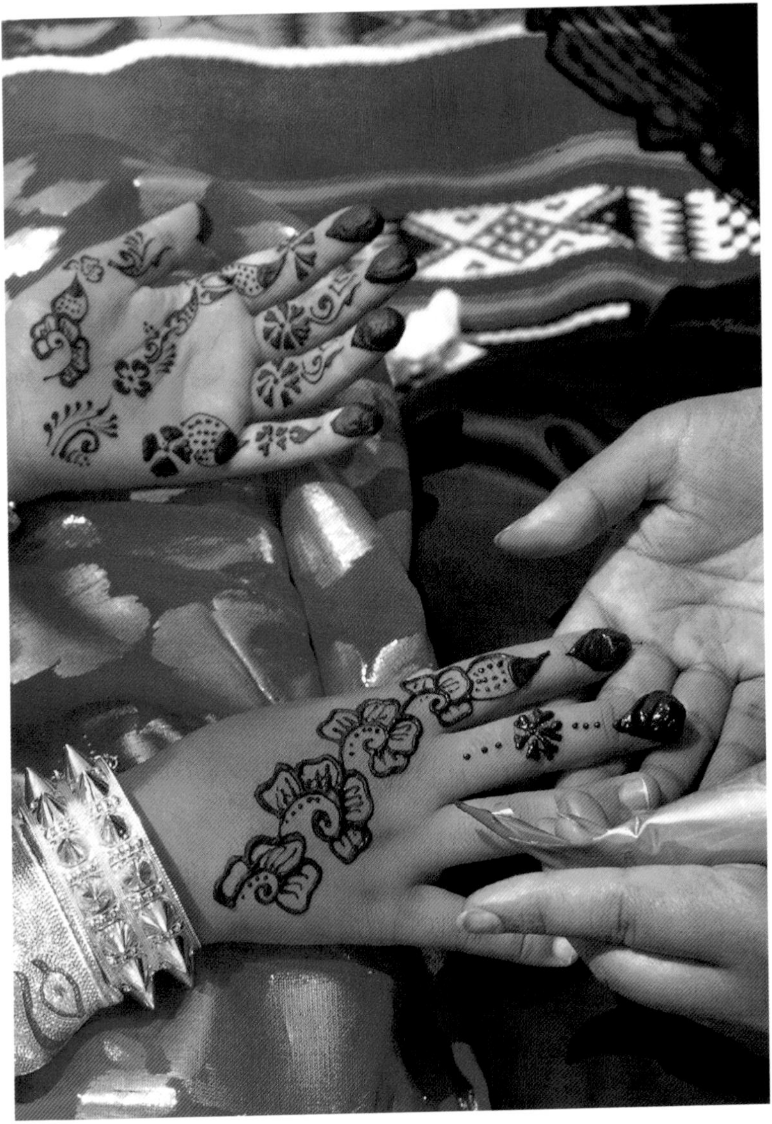

APPLICATION TECHNIQUES

A woman from the United Arab Emirates has henna applied for her wedding.

Safety

Henna has been used in its various forms for thousand of years, and, because it is a completely natural product, allergic reactions are extremely rare. If you are concerned about having an adverse reaction, or know that you have particularly sensitive skin, I suggest you do a sample skin test. Apply a small amount of henna paste to an inconspicuous patch of skin, scrape it off, and wait for 24 hours. If there has been no reaction, you are safe to proceed. This precaution also applies to the use of essential oils: remember to use them only in their diluted form.

Getting Started

Before looking at ways of applying your henna, it is important to create the right environment and to have the right equipment ready.

When you are mixing henna, you should use a bowl that you are happy to use only for that purpose. Remember, henna is a dye and will stain any surface with which it comes into contact. Consequently, you should protect any surfaces you will be working on as well as your own clothing. I always mix and apply henna over the kitchen sink; it is easy to wash off from the sink surface and you are close to the tap if necessary!

Tools You Will Need

There are several possible tools for applying henna to the skin, the most common of which is a plastic cone. These are often provided with bags of henna powder, or if not, it is very easy to make your own using disposable pastry bags, or zip-lock plastic bags that you can get from a stationer. Fill the bag with the henna paste, roll it up into a cone shape, and secure it with tape. Then snip off a tiny part of the point to create the hole through which to squeeze the paste. If you cut too big a hole, don't worry. Fold over the edge of the cone and wrap the tip with sticky tape to make the hole smaller.

Pre-mixed henna that comes in a tube should have a nozzle so you can apply it straight from the tube. This is the easiest method for

An Indian woman demonstrates the use of a cone for applying henna.

beginners, and we have provided you with such a tube in this kit.

The most traditional tool for applying henna is a fine wooden stick. The modern equivalent would be an orange stick used for nail care, and they are easily available from any chemist. The sticks have a fine point that is ideal for applying thin lines and intricate henna designs.

One method I have seen in some Asian countries is to use a syringe (without the needle, of course). This is filled with henna and slowly drizzled on to the skin in the desired pattern. You should be able to find a suitable syringe in the medicine section of a pet shop. These syringes are used for dosing kittens and puppies with medicine, but are also ideal for applying henna!

I recommend that you always have an orange stick or cotton buds to hand for touch-ups and minor corrections. A toothpick, wet wipes or damp cotton wool are also handy. Once your design has been applied, you will also need some lemon juice, sugar, and a utensil such as an old butter knife for scraping off the dried henna (see page 41).

This Moroccan artist prefers to apply henna with a finely pointed instrument.

Skin Preparation

Henna actually stains the top layer of skin, so it is essential to prepare the skin properly. Cleaning the skin removes dead skin cells, which will help the design to adhere for longer. First clean the area with soap and water, then swab the skin with alcohol. Alternatively, you may like to swab the skin with orange flower water or rose water, a method used in Morocco.

After cleaning the skin, it is recommended that you wipe the skin with eucalyptus oil; this opens the pores so that the henna can stain the skin more thoroughly. It also helps to disguise the distinctive smell of henna. Please note that essential oils are very strong, and should be diluted in a base oil or water before direct application to the skin.

You are now ready to start.

Applying Henna to the Skin

This is the moment you have been waiting for! Now is the time for your creativity to flow. The main requirement, however, is a steady hand. Make sure the henna is the consistency of toothpaste. This will enable you to control the rate at which you apply the henna. Drizzle the henna lightly on to the skin as if you were applying icing to a cake. Take care not to apply too much at once as it will spread and could easily be smudged. The following pages look at the different ways in which to create your designs.

36

Using a Transfer

Transfers are an excellent way to apply certain types of designs, and I highly recommend these for beginners or those who do not have a particularly steady hand. We have provided some transfers for you to use in this kit. With transfers you do not have the complication of peeling away a stencil that could disturb your design (see page 38).

First of all, rub your skin with oil. Next, place the transfer over this area, and gently tap the back of the transfer all over with your finger. This leaves an impression of the transfer on the skin. Finally, carefully peel away the transfer, leaving the design for you to paint over with henna paste.

You can buy transfers from the usual outlets (see page 21), but it is very easy to make your own. Photocopy the design of your choice from the last section of this book (see page 44) to the size that you want it to appear on your skin. Place the photocopy on the skin, ink side down. Then rub over the back of the paper with acetone or nail polish remover. This transfers the design on to the skin, which you paint over with the henna paste.

This method is particularly good for intricate designs with fine lines because the transfer ink will not show through the henna. But I would not recommend it for designs that involve solid blocks of colour or heavy lines.

Using a Stencil

This employs the same principle as stencils that are used in home decorating. With a stencil, you simply fill in the gaps with the henna paste. Some stencils create very intricate designs which is useful if you do not yet have the skill to apply these patterns freehand. A vast range of stencils is available from Asian supermarkets. They may come specifically in the shape of hands and feet, continuous designs for ankle or arm bands, or paisley and floral motifs that can be placed just about anywhere on the body.

You can make your own stencils using waxproof paper or very thin waxed card. Draw or photocopy your design on to the card, and cut out the relief (the sections where you want the henna to appear), using an art knife. You now have your own custom-made stencil.

Place the template on to the skin, and fill in the exposed sections of skin with henna. Once you have completed this, slowly peel away the stencil, taking great care not to disturb the henna. Your design is now complete, and you just have to wait for the paste to dry.

Freehand Application

This method is for the more advanced practitioner and demands a certain degree of artistic ability and flair. The most important requirements for this type of application, however, are a steady hand and an eye for detail.

When I do freehand designs, I usually have a picture beside me of the design I am going to recreate on the skin. This is a very rewarding way of applying henna and allows great scope for your creativity. If you have ever seen an expert applying henna tattoos, they will almost certainly have done so freehand. It is fascinating to watch, and a great way to pick up useful tips and techniques. I would recommend this method only if you already have a certain amount of experience using henna; the chances of making a mistake are much higher and, as you will find out, they are not always easy to correct or remove.

40

This design is being applied freehand, working up from the wrist to the fingertips.

Happy with your Design?

Whichever method of application you have used – transfer, stencil or freehand – you need to leave the paste on the skin for at least four or five hours. Eight hours is actually the ideal period, but this may not always be convenient with hand and feet designs. The longer you leave the paste on the skin, the stronger the colour will be, and the longer the design will last. Some people suggest that you wrap the designs in bandages and leave the henna on overnight, but I find this inconvenient and unnecessary. It is essential, however, that you plan ahead when creating your henna designs, and leave enough time for the henna to develop properly – otherwise, all your efforts will be wasted.

The longer the henna paste stays moist, the deeper will be the final colour, so according to your taste, you should now apply a solution of two parts lemon juice to one part sugar to moisten it. The henna will flake off naturally as it dries, but try to keep it moist for at least four to five hours. When the dried henna flakes off, your design will be revealed underneath. To assist in the removal of the dried henna, you could use a butter knife or toothpick. I cannot stress enough the importance of leaving the henna on the skin for the correct amount of time. The longer you leave it, the deeper the colour of the tattoo, and the greater its durability. So remember – patience is a virtue, and plan your time accordingly.

Problems?

If you follow all the instructions above carefully, you should not encounter any problems with your henna tattoo. There are some tips I can offer, however, should you have any minor accidents.

The most common problem is making a mistake in the design or splashing henna in the wrong place by accident. If you act quickly, you can remove the excess henna from the skin before it has a chance to stain. Do this with a toothpick if it is in a tricky area; you can also use wipes or damp cotton wool to clean other areas. But if the henna is not removed immediately, some stain may remain.

Once your tattoo has developed, if you find that you do not like it, unfortunately there is not a lot you can do. All I can suggest is that you scrub the area vigorously with soap and water, which will help the tattoo to lift off a lot more quickly. But since henna is a dye that penetrates the skin, even with persistent cleaning, it may take several days to remove.

Aftercare

Once all these steps are completed and you are happy with your design, there are a few measures you can take to enhance the durability of your motif.

● You should not expose the area to water for at least twelve hours. You should also avoid saunas, since this encourages the regeneration of your skin. Do not scrub the area too vigorously when bathing, since this will remove the skin cells that contain the henna stain.

● You may find that the stain will deepen slightly over the few days following the application. If you wish to deepen the colour further, you can rub some mustard oil over the design.

● Moisturize the area regularly, though not more than twice daily. This will help to slow down your skin's natural regeneration process. Make sure the area is totally dry before putting on your clothes, or your garments may get stained.

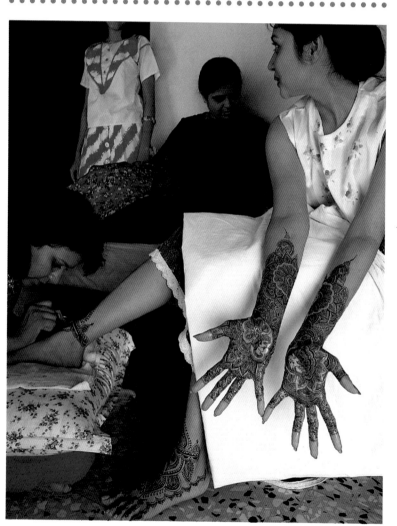

A bride has her feet painted while she waits patiently for her hand designs to dry.

DESIGNS

• •

O n the following pages, you will find
lots of beautiful and inspiring
designs, ranging from quite simple
patterns to the very intricate. The most
traditional are specifically for the hands
and feet, while others are motifs that
could be applied almost anywhere – the
arm, shoulder, tummy, hip or ankle. You
could use these designs as templates for
making your own stencils and transfers or,
if you feel confident enough, you could
copy them freehand. Whatever the
occasion and whichever feature you
wish to decorate, you are sure to find
something to suit among these stunning
and eye-catching designs.

48

51

52

54

56

58

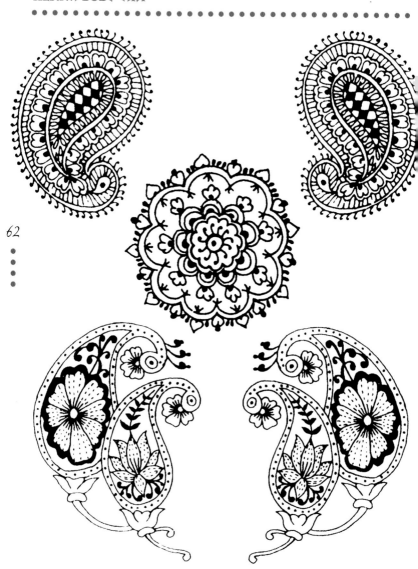

INDEX

Numbers in italics refer to pictures.